ARA

A Monkey Puzzle Tree Tale

Ladey Adey

Additional material
Abbirose Adey

Ladey Adey

Endorsements

How inspiring it is reading Ladey's book. A romantic author in the content and writing, modern in the way of investigating. Her information surprises me, despite having researched a lot about this tree, in addition to living in the Araucaria forests of the Andean Araucania region of Chile. Certainly, the British Islands are the best second home for the Monkey Puzzle Tree, for which the story of 'Ara', is a beautiful complement to the botanical and cultural virtues of this species.

Rodrigo Fernández, Film-maker and Author: *Chilean Trees Around the World*

Ladey has certainly provided a great solution to the puzzle of the Araucaria araucana tree, which grows in a land without monkeys, and whose fruit are nuts, in this entertaining narrative.

Bruce Roberts, Author: *The Godot Orange*

What a joyful book! Ladey has packed this work with love, detail and it sparkles with the personality of the Monkey Puzzle itself. It makes me feel almost benevolent towards a tree that I once got irretrievably stuck under while surveying a gardens!

Sarah Owen-Hughes, Head Gardener - Rudding Park Hotel

Can you imagine a world without trees? I can...but it's a dejecting image. We need to celebrate trees more, not just for the vast array of ecosystem services they provide (completely free of charge), nor even for the beauty they bring to our world or the health benefits they offer, but also for the creativity they inspire within us. Being around trees simply brings out the best in us and Ladey celebrates Araucaria in the most wonderful and delightful way. A fitting tribute for this unique and uplifting tree.

Gerry O'Brien, Ecotherapist, Sustainability Consultant and Author: *Wildlife Whispers*

ARA

A Monkey Puzzle Tree Tale

The fictional story of an Araucaria Tree - The Quintessential British Branch!

Ladey Adey

Foreword by David Gedye
Author: Araucaria the Monkey Puzzle

Ladey Adey

COPYRIGHT

Copyright ©2023 by Ladey Adey

Published: April 22nd 2023 by Ladey Adey Publications, Ancaster, Lincolnshire UK.

Ladey Adey has asserted her right to be identified as the author of this Work in accordance with the Copyright, Designs and Patents Act 1988.

ISBN: 978-1-913579-38-8 (Hardback)

ISBN: 978-1-913579-39-5 (Electronic)

Coming soon in Audio.

All rights reserved. No part of this publication may be reproduced, stored in a retrieval system, or transmitted in any form or by any means—for example, electronic, photocopy, recording—without the prior written permission of the publisher. The only exception is brief quotations in printed reviews.

British Library Cataloguing-in-Publication Data. A catalogue record for this book is available from The British Library.

Editor: Abbirose Adey, of Ladey Adey Publications.

Cover Design by Abbirose Adey, of Ladey Adey Publications.

The author and publisher has made every effort to ensure the external websites included in this book are correct and up to date at the time of going to press. The author and publisher are not responsible for the content, quality or continuing accessibility of the sites.

Note: Facts are in the story, the author has taken the liberty of fictionalizing story, conversations and speech.

Please leave a review on Amazon for Ladey.

Ara: A Monkey Puzzle Tree Tale

DEDICATION

To Denis Peter Adey, my husband and forever friend who started me off on my Araucaria journey with his love of the Monkey Puzzle Tree. Whilst travelling in the car whenever we passed a garden sporting such a tree, the cry would sound, *"Monkey Puzzle!?!"*

He now has his own *Araucaria araucana*, which at the time of writing this tale is about two and half feet tall and has pride of place in our garden. It pricks us every time we get near it!

To my Mum, Doris Shaw, who loved all plants and trees. In later years, when her sight failed she could be found 'weeding' using a magnifying glass! A true and beloved gardener whose advice will be sorely missed.

Finally, to all Monkey Puzzle Tree fans who have kindly sent me pictures of their trees and stories about them. I've cried at the stories I've heard; people returning home to find their beloved Monkey Puzzle tree cut down in its prime because another member of the household wanted more space or light!

I've cried with laughter at other stories and I don't mind whether they're true or myth. They are all good in my book! Keep sending them to me please - here is my email: ladey@ladeyadey.com.

Ladey Adey

In Memory

For all the Araucaria trees
which have been felled prematurely
in their home country and worldwide.

Contents

Dedication v
Foreword xi
Part One 1
    The Story of Ara 3
    Migration Across Continents 4
    So Magnificent and Majestic Are We 5
    Pia 6
    Jesus 7
    Molina, Dombey and the Don 8
    Archibald Menzies 9
    James Macrae 10
    King William IV 11
    Kew Gardens 12
    Lord and Lady Grenville 13
    Sir William Molesworth 14
    Queen Victoria and Prince Albert 15
    William Lobb 16
    First Nurserymen 17
    Philip Frost 18
    David Gedye 19
    Whitby Jet 20
    Captain Tremlett 21
    Pablo Neruda 22
    You, Dear Reader 23

Part Two 25
   In Love with Monkey Puzzle Trees 27
   Modern Stories 29
   Myth, Superstition or Fact 33
   Monkey Puzzle in the Arts and Literature . 39
   Recommended Books 41
   Websites Worth Seeing 53
   Monkey Puzzle Fun 57
About the Author 67
   Other Books by Ladey 69
Index 71
Your Notes 75

Ara: A Monkey Puzzle Tree Tale

**Ask the animals,
and they will teach you,**

**or the birds in the sky,
and they will tell you;**

**or speak to the earth,
and it will teach you,**

**or let the fish in the sea
inform you.**

**In His hand is the life
of every creature
and the breath of all mankind.**

Job 12:7-8, 10 (NIV Bible)

Ladey Adey

David Gedye, Benmore (RBGE Garden)

Foreword

Of all the trees which grow in the British Isles, the Monkey Puzzle is the definitive - once seen, once named, never to be forgotten - tree.

From the moment you ask, *"What is this tree called?"* to hearing the answer, *"Araucaria araucana, The Monkey Puzzle"*, you will never mix up the Monkey Puzzle with any other tree, nor will you ever forget the tree's common name. Yet, it is also a *'Marmite®'* tree. You either love it or hate it - or perhaps there is a little sliver of middle ground where you can admire it from a distance, but don't want to get too close to its very prickly leaves.

Ladey Adey knows which camp she is in. Her love of the tree comes across in every chapter of this delightful little book which narrates - from the tree's perspective - the story of its journey from the time of the dinosaurs to its establishment in parks and gardens across the British Isles.

Is it because the tree is so unusual it seems to stimulate curiosity in all who like and admire it? Ladey's curiosity has done more than motivate her to write a story - it has taken her on a journey. In the *'Sites Worth Seeing'* section, she introduces the reader to a sample of the information to be found in YouTube videos and internet articles.

For those willing to search the internet, there is a wealth of information on how to germinate the seed and care for the tree, and a range of delicious recipes which use the edible kernels as a core ingredient. Regrettably, as Monkey Puzzle kernels aren't readily available in our shops, you either need to have your own tree, or know of a tree where you can gather fresh seed and extract the kernels; you may have to get up early in the morning to beat the mice, squirrels and birds!

Ladey's curiosity extended even further when she discovered and then created a list of the pubs and restaurants who have Monkey Puzzle in their name.

After reading this light-hearted foreword to the story of Ara, you might be motivated to participate in the conservation of the species which, like so many living things on our planet, is under threat from climate change and other factors.

David Gedye
(September 2022)

Author: Araucaria the Monkey Puzzle

Part One

The Story of Ara

**Look deep into nature,
and then you will understand
everything better.**

Albert Einstein

ARA

Hello! My friends call me Ara, short for Araucaria; my cheeky friends call me Monkey and this is my tale...

Life began for my ancestors, the Araucaria araucana species, millions of years ago. This included my cousins, of which I have at least 40, including the *Bunya Bunya Tree* in Australia and *Klinky* in Papua New Guinea. My ancestors started their global travel as the Pangea landmass broke into the continents as you know them today. So, we are spread widely over the globe.

This occurred about 335 million years ago in the late Paleozoic and early Mesozoic eras. Our species can live individually for 2,000 years which gives us a lot of memories! We are the first of our kind and even today are called, *'a living fossil!'*

We allowed the dinosaurs to feed on our leaves and branches for their dinner. Later, we moved our branches so high it meant only the Diplodocus could reach them! It gave us happiness to sustain such creatures, for their moment in history.

Ara says,
"Our history is fascinating.
We knew the world from the moment
the Spirit of God hovered over
the face of the water."

Ladey Adey

MIGRATION ACROSS CONTINENTS

Continental drift conditions were not always perfect for my ancestors but this phenomenon has played a significant role in the evolution and survival of many species over millions of years.

As the Earth's landmasses shifted, certain conditions became more or less favourable for different forms of life. For example, during the ice ages of the northern hemisphere, many of my ancestors perished in the harsh, frozen conditions. However, those who were able to migrate and adapt to the southern hemisphere, where the climate was warmer, were able to survive and thrive. We all like a little warmth!

Among these survivors were my ancestors, the Araucaria trees; a Chilean survivor. Today, we have over 20 species of Araucaria still surviving in the southern hemisphere. We are one of the most well-known of these species and I am proud to say I was adopted as the National Tree of Chile.

Overall, the survival of the Araucaria trees and their various species is a testament to the resilience and adaptability of life on Earth, even in the face of shifting continents and changing climates.

Ara says,
"God's hand is at work helping
humans to find many Araucarias
in their future."

So Magnificant And Majestic Are We

We were created to be majestic, yet humble, evergreen trees. We belong to the genus of conifers and grow up over 165 ft (50m) tall, extending our branches many feet wide. Our towering presence has often been a source of wonder for humans. At our highest, we can even reach Admiral Horatio Nelson's shoulder high up on the column in Trafalgar Square, London. Our hexagonal bark is a dusky grey colour and our vibrant, prickly leaves are '*Fibonacci-ally*' arranged. These leaves are famous for their crowded, overlapping, tough nature, ending in a point, and they are commented on by everyone who meets us.

We loved to interact with humans who were captivated by our beauty and we found ways of helping them by producing nuts for nourishment, and giving our strong timber to build ships and other structures. We have even been used as status symbols. Our remains, formed under the pressure of earth and water, have created precious gemstones, still collected today.

We continue to thrive in the wild, providing a vital source of oxygen to the planet and supporting countless species with our presence. Our resilience and adaptability have allowed us to survive for millions of years and with the help of our human friends.

Ara says,
"Humans can be enterprising creatures!"

Pia

As an Araucaria tree, my spirit has been passed down through generations, ensuring I am ever-present within every tree of my species. One of the most memorable human interactions was with a young offshoot who had just turned 50 years old, finally old enough to produce seeds and kernels. This special moment occurred with a Chilean beauty of the indigenous Mapuche tribe.

Her name was Pia, she was using a stone sling to shake the branches for the kernels, filled with nuts, to drop. Pia's family had their own valley of trees. As Pia gathered my fruit, she sang an enchanting melody about how delicious my seeds were and how she would choose to cook them in a sweet broth or roast them over the fire with some animal fat dripping on top of them. She sang to her beloved Pehuén,

"For my family, I come to collect
Ara's seeds, majestic architect.
Delicious cooked, roasted or in a sweet broth,
and sucked as raw, yet I do give my troth.
To leave some behind, For the earth to protect"

Pia's love and appreciation for the bounty I provided was a humbling and heart-warming experience. Pia, and her tribe loved me, appreciated all I gave and wanted to ensure the survival of my future generations.

Ara says,
"Humans can be inquisitive and sweet creatures."

JESUS

I was surprised when our surplus seeds became a favourite food for mankind. As we multiplied, the seeds became part of the local people's staple diet. They came back time and time again though they did complain about getting pricked! Some would even gather round my trunk and tell stories.

Once they talked about a man named Jesus who healed the sick and told stories of his own, which have travelled across the world reaching every generation throughout history. Here is a favourite story told around my trunk.

"I've just been told about the large crowds who gathered to hear Jesus speak, sometimes as many as 5,000 people. They would stay for hours, prepared to miss a meal rather than miss one word! But Jesus didn't want them to go hungry. When he asked how much food there was left, he was told 'two loaves of bread and five fish' but the young boy who had these was willing to share. Miraculously, Jesus multiplied these for everyone! I believe if they had bread using ground Araucaria seeds they would have fed everyone!"

Once a group member said, *"I'm so sad about Jesus' death, especially when he had a crown of thorns put on his head."* It got very sombre and I heaved a sigh of relief that one of my spikes had not been used to make this wreath of humility!

I keep all the stories I hear within me and like the trees in the field 'clap my hands when I recall them!

Ara says,
"Humans can be talkative creatures."

Molina, Dombey & The Don

As I watched our saplings grow, it was exciting to see how humans viewed us. Luis de Molina, a Jesuit priest and botanist called me, *"The most beautiful tree of Chile"* and became excited about telling the world. I was featured within his manuscripts.

Molina was exiled to Italy but continued to share his work across Europe. This led to many expeditions to Chile by botanists, physicians and explorers.

We were visited by Joseph Dombey, a botanist, who became really excited about our wood. He said,

"I must tell the world about this amazing tree". Dombey was assistant to Don Francisco Dendariarena, a Spanish explorer, who arrived and exclaimed, *"Si si, this timber will be superb for our shipbuilding!"* Consequently, logging began and much of our wood was used to repair the Spanish fleet.

I had enjoyed Molina sharing his fervour for my species. How he raved at the strength and uniqueness of my wood. However, it saddened me to know those who followed, like the Don, used me to build their warships and watched as many members of my family were destroyed without ceremony or replanting!

Surprisingly, someone chose to preserve a little of my wood from a ship once displayed in the British Museum!

Ara says,
"Humans can be destructive creatures."

Ara: A Monkey Puzzle Tree Tale

ARCHIBALD MENZIES

My species were documented in drawings and writings, plus discussed until they came to the attention of the world. When our seeds and cuttings began to travel the world, life was very exciting. We were classified as a conifer and our seeds travelled the seven seas!

Famous gardens (such as Kew Gardens in London) were given some seedlings, thanks to Archibald Menzies, an Assistant Surgeon in the Royal Navy with a passion for plants with medicinal purposes. On one trip, he met with Ambrosio O´Higgins, an Irishman, who arrived in South America as a soldier and became a Governor of Chile.

As with the custom of the day, the Araucaria kernels were a popular food and trees were plentiful. Menzies remembers, *"The Governor, over dinner, regaled me with the story of this incredible tree, native to Chile with its distinctive branches, a 'grand' tree. As a speciality, we were given some cooked seeds - they tasted like chestnuts. I was so excited and wanted to arrange a trip to see the tree for myself, but tide waits for no man and we had to continue our journey. Before I left, I was given some seeds as a momento and popped them into my pocket for safe-keeping. Later, I propagated them on board ship. Once home, I shared these seedlings with my friend, Sir Joseph Banks, of Isleworth, gave five to Kew Gardens and some to others who were collectors with a range of rare and exotic specimens."*

Ara says,
"Humans can be industrious creatures."

Ladey Adey

JAMES MACRAE

A plant collector for The Horticultural Society, (rivals with Kew) James Macrae, played a crucial role in the growth and introduction of my kind to gardens across the British Isles. Macrae's method involved growing the trees from seed, which required a significant level of attention and expertise.

James said, *"Most people associate me as a botanist, famous for collecting plants from the Sandwich Islands, but sometimes trips took me to other parts of the world. While on HMS Blonde, on a scheduled visit to Chile, I was to see the most fascinating of specimens including the Chilean geranium, and the never to be forgotten, seed of the Araucaria Tree, the latter was challenging to grow."*

One reason I'm hard to grow is I have an astonishing approach to reproduction. My species have male and female trees, which produce different-looking seed pods. However, it is not possible to work out if I'm male or female until I produce my first fruit! This means, to successfully grow the trees from seed, both male and female trees needed to be present to enable fertilisation. This concept was different from what humans were accustomed to, as they often assumed only one tree was necessary for seed germination.

God in his creation really knew what he was doing and as the saying goes, it takes two to tango! The seeds need to be together for pollination. It took a while for the humans to work this out!

Ara says,
"Humans can be persistent creatures."

Ara: A Monkey Puzzle Tree Tale

King William IV

I still remember the day King William IV himself took notice of me. It was a moment of great pride and honour for me, as I knew this distinction was not given to many plants. King William had the nickname 'Sailor King' as he served in the Royal Navy, and was Britain's Lord High Admiral. He captained the HMS Pegasus and HMS Andromeda and travelled over the North American East Coast and the Caribbean Sea, where he would have had many conversations with doctors, often specialists in botany.

He was gifted one of my species (I believe it was through his connections at Kew rather than through his sea-faring trips) and loved my unique qualities; my hardiness, ability to thrive and use for timber. Or, maybe it was my striking appearance which impressed him most.

Regardless of the reason, the King's interest in me was not without reward. He was known for his generosity and was not shy in sharing his treasures. In fact, he offered to give away Buckingham Palace, his very own residence, twice! Once to be used as a barracks, and the second time as a replacement for the Houses of Parliament when it was destroyed in a fire in 1830. The King gifted one of his Araucaria trees, it was 5 ft tall and grown in a tub, to Lord and Lady Grenville. It was planted in their Dropmore Garden, Buckinghamshire and eventually grew to over 50 ft.

Ara says,
"Humans can be generous creatures."

Ladey Adey

KEW GARDENS

Life wasn't easy for the first seedling trees brought to Britain by Menzies and the nurserymen at Kew had their work cut out. They called me a Pine (Araucaria imbricata) and had to find the best way of caring and growing-them-on with the knowledge they had at the time. Just planting out the seedling trees wasn't good enough and a couple died.

They were then kept in the glasshouses to give warmth and shelter from the British weather. The quick growing trees still presented a problem which wasn't helped by a misguided ingenious idea of two footmen! It began at a Gala Party at Carlton House; eager to please, the footmen discussed how to make the Gala memorable.

"I know what we can do, let's place the lanterns on the branches of this tree, they won't fall off because the shape will keep them in. I've got a ladder and we can put them on the lowest branches – we can light the candles at nightfall and it'll create a beautiful picture. We can call it the Candelabra tree." They snickered and nudged one another.

It did indeed look great, but the lanterns burnt my branches, in fact fire is the one thing which I'm terrified of and has caused much damage to my species over the years. When those at Kew saw me, they said, *"Oh No! This tree is irretrievably injured - WHO DID THIS? We will have to concentrate on growing the other seedlings."*

Ara says,
"Humans can be horticultural creatures."

Ara: A Monkey Puzzle Tree Tale

LORD AND LADY GRENVILLE

As the "Monkey Puzzle Tree," I quickly became a beloved and sought-after specimen in the eyes of the British aristocracy. Some loved our quirky branches and unique appearance, while others despised our prickly nature. Nevertheless, it became quite fashionable to have us on important estates or as a specimen tree in a Pinetum. We quickly became a status symbol for the landed gentry, and nothing was more impressive than an avenue of trees.

Those who owned us sought to immortalize our beauty in various ways. For instance, Lord and Lady Grenville of Dropmore had a reputation for their show garden and collection of rare trees, planted as a Pinetum. Their Araucaria tree, was one of many grown on the estate and attracted visits from travellers including Mr Downing from a international horticultural society, who wrote a paper entitled, 'Letters from England'.

Lady Grenville, was so enamoured with her Monkey Puzzle Trees she commissioned William Richardson, Member of the Royal Academy of Arts, to paint one of them. She said, *"This tree has such a special place in my heart and its strength and beauty needs to be captured."*

This was a testament to the special place we held in the hearts of our owners.

Ara says,
"Humans can be prickly creatures."

Ladey Adey

SIR WILLIAM MOLESWORTH

The myth of our new name was coined in 1834 when Mary Ford's brother, Sir William Molesworth MP and Secretary of State for the Colonies, surprised the family with an Araucaria tree and asked Mary to help show it off. He said, *"It was the best surprise I could arrange. It was a memory from the colonies, a tree my sister and others will never see in its natural setting. The fee was an expensive and extravagant £30!"*

Mary arranged for the planting ceremony during a house party at her brother's Pencarrow Estate, in Cornwall. One of the guests, Charles Austin, an eminent barrister, looked at the branches and said,

"How funny, with the prickliness and leathery feel of the leaves, the different shapes of the branches, I'd say it would be a puzzle even for a monkey."

The fable stuck, was retold and we have been called a Monkey Puzzle Tree ever since! It has a French translation, The Monkey Despair (Désespoir des Singes), though this myth says it was named before Charles Austin's comment!

Sir William Molesworth didn't stop with one of my species, he actually planted an avenue of them, in excess of sixty trees and supported many of the nurseries in buying their seeds and plants!

Ara says,
"Humans can be humorous creatures."

Ara: A Monkey Puzzle Tree Tale

Queen Victoria and Prince Albert

The Victorians were fascinated with our appearance. Queen Victoria and Prince Albert saw my descendants in the Dropmore Gardens and like many, were in awe. The Queen asked for a tree as a present for Albert, it duly arrived and was planted in Windsor Castle Garden. Prince Albert said, *"These trees would make fine Christmas Trees, celebrating the birth of Jesus and it would be fun to decorate them but they are so prickly, I'd fear for the safety of children."*

So, this honour went to the *Yew* and later transferred to another pine conifer the *Fir*.

Prince Albert was courageous in his encouragement of industry and new invention, he realised my gemstones (jet) could be used. He helped those trading in it when he ensured it was part of the Great Exhibition of 1851.

Queen Victoria loved the tree and one still stands in one of Buckingham Palace Gardens. When she had to say a, too soon, farewell to her beloved husband she took to wearing jewellery made from Whitby Jet. In 1861, at the funeral of Albert, Victoria wore a Whitby Jet brooch as part of her mourning dress. Naturally, this set a fashion among the 'le bon ton', endorsing another use of my ancestors.

Ara says,
"Humans can be courageous creatures."

Ladey Adey

William Lobb

My ancestors became more than specimen trees or only seen in large estates thanks to the growing number of nurserymen. William Lobb was one such plant hunter and collector, who supplied the seed to Veitch's Nursery of Exeter and enabled the public's growing interest too.

William says, *"Travelling may be a great adventure but it is often gruelling. To find the Araucaria, I travelled overland to Chile and over the Andes. I thought this would save me the perilous sea voyage around Cape Horn but the Mountain range included navigating over five foot deep snow, frozen so hard the mules made no impression and the cold was intense. I collapsed, ill with fever many times.*

Finally, I reached the Araucania region where the Araucaria grew on ridges but the cones containing the seeds were well out of reach. They were magnificent to behold and I knew my employers in Britian would want their own stock. A quick and easy way to gather the seeds came to me as I felt my trusty gun at my side. I took aim and fired! I shot the cones from the trees then sent my porters in to gather them for me. It was good fun as I was a good shot. Now, I was able to collect over 3,000 seeds, which I personally saw onto a ship and sent to England. I knew Veitch Nursery made a profit as they sold the seedlings for £10 per 100."

Ara says,
"Humans can be over enthusiastic, energetic, and 'gung-ho' creatures!"

Ara: A Monkey Puzzle Tree Tale

First Nurserymen

Where the rich and famous set trends others will follow. Myths are often generated during advertisements including claims for history. Veitch predicted the horticultural fashion would enable everyone to have an Ara of their own.

Other nurseries were enterprising and pandered to gardening trends such as Youells of Great Yarmouth who received a Royal Warrant from Dowager Queen Adelaide (Widow of King William IV). Suppliers of botanic seeds included, Skirving of Liverpool, Lucombe & Pince of Exeter and Loddiges of Hackney.

In 1866, Veitch's son, Robert T Veitch, planted a Monkey Puzzle tree in *Higher Cemetery,* Exeter. Many of this horticultural family rest in this cemetery.

Kew is one of the most famous depositories of plants and seeds, keeping millions of seeds safe. In 2009, Joanna Wenham, one of Kew's staff from Wakefield (Sussex), went on an expedition to Chile with seed bank partners INIA and UK Forestry Commission. Joanna says, *"We brought back more than half a million seeds from 80 different species of plants from the expedition. Those species which are not able to be stored in the seed bank such as Araucaria araucana, were propagated for planting and will be conserved in the landscape at Wakehurst. So far, over 40 trees have been planted."*

I imagine this new avenue at Wakehurst is similar to walking up a Chilean mountain side.

Ara says,
"Humans can be competitive creatures."

Ladey Adey

Philip Frost

The Victorian era in England was a time for innovation and development in horticulture. During this period, the country saw a surge in interest in gardening and landscaping, leading to the rise of a new profession: the head gardener.

Head gardeners were responsible for managing and maintaining the vast gardens and estates, popular among the wealthy elite of the time. They were skilled experts in a range of areas, from horticulture and landscaping to irrigation and machinery.

Philip Frost, started as under-gardener and later took the role of Head Gardener, of the Dropmore Pinetum, Buckinghamshire. Here, he had the privilege of caring for one of my descendants to ensure it thrived and remained healthy.

Philip was a passionate advocate for the Monkey Puzzle Tree, germinating the seeds in a tin carried in his waistcoat pocket, writing about them for newspapers, magazines and books.

Philip said, *"It is with pleasure I send this picture to The Gardener's Chronicle. It is the first photograph of the Araucaria in the UK, please note the tree looks better than me! I've enclosed an article giving insight and information about the Araucaria Tree. The picture shows the beautiful specimen which I've had the honour to care for as part of my work on the Dropmore Estate."*

Ara says,
"Humans can be visual creatures."

Ara: A Monkey Puzzle Tree Tale

DAVID GEDYE

Before long, many gardens throughout the world had one of my descendants in their garden. They are beloved by their owners and kept in great regard. Public houses and some businesses have been named after me and I've been featured in a children's book about a Little Unicorn discovering the dinosaurs!

Philip Frost's great, great grandson, David Gedye, wrote a book dedicated to me.

David said, *"The Monkey Puzzle Tree contains so much history and many memories. My own memories include stories my mother and grandmother told me about my great-great grandfather. My grandmother ensured I inherited the Philip Frost photographs so it makes sense I should feature many of them in my book dedicated to this most majestic, yet humble, of all trees."*

It is fascinating how much influence I've had on people and their journey's in life and David's book, *Araucaria The Monkey Puzzle,* is quoted widely as it is recognised as the definitive book on my history and life.

David travels widely giving presentations on the Araucaria and visits estates where the original trees were brought to the UK. The latest visit was to Benmore Estate in Scotland which has 300 trees. He is always available to share his knowledge, and dispel myths associated with the Monkey Puzzle. The author of this book was privileged to interview David on her podcast: the *Ladey Adey Show*.

Ara says,
"Humans can be vivacious creatures."

Ladey Adey

Whitby Jet

We go a full circle as the enduring uses for our wood continue though the use of our remains! We have formed a gemstone. Whitby Jet is a highly valued gemstone formed from the remains of ancient trees. Our fossilised wood from the Araucariaceae family of trees which grew in the region of Whitby, a small town in North Yorkshire, England.

Over millions of years, the organic matter from the trees underwent a process of carbonisation, intense heat and pressure. Hey, we were even the precursor to coal. This makes our species valued for its historical and geological significance.

We have formed into a hard or soft black jet or black amber but it has more elasticity than most jets meaning it can be cut and carved. When humans mine or collect our jet from the cliffs and shores they cut it making sure not to damage it and give it a polish. The black gemstone has a lustre shine and is warm to touch; I like to think this passes on our memories. It was even mined in the Bronze age and turned into jewellery and artefacts. We did have a heyday in the Victorian age especially as our deep, black colour was associated with mourning!

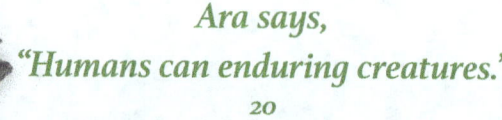

Ara says,
"Humans can enduring creatures."

Ara: A Monkey Puzzle Tree Tale

Captain Tremlett

The process by which organic matter can be transformed into a precious and enduring gemstone was aided by the meeting of Robert Jefferson, a painter, and an inn keeper, John Carter, who lived in Haggersgate, Whitby. They had their own cottage industry where they carved crosses and beads selling them for as much as one pound and one shilling.

Captain Tremlett, a naval pensioner settled in the area and whilst exploring his new community saw their work. As an enterprising, retired Naval Officer he realised the potential of their work and struck up a conversation. He saw the method they were using; a time consuming, hand-cutting of the stones with knives and files. He said, *"We could do much more if we use a lathe and go into production to produce jewellery and trinkets. Let me show you some jet beads which have been turned in this way."*

The trio spoke with a local turner, named Matthew Hill, and employed him to make jewellery using his lathe. Consequently, 'Jet Jewellery' was born and became the biggest trade in Whitby. It is still going today under the name W. Hamond but it's strapline is 'The Original Whitby Jet Shop Est 1860'.

I am delighted the author of this book received an everyday present, a necklace of Whitby Jet in the shape of a tree, by her husband as a thank you for writing my story.

Ara says,
"Humans can be preservatious creatures."

Ladey Adey

Pablo Neruda

A major influencer in the 20th Century for my species was Pablo Neruda, a Chilean poet with a propensity for politics. Over time he became known around the world. He was awarded many Peace Prizes, and in 1971, the Nobel Prize in Literature. What a guy! His *Ode to Araucaria araucana*, shares an emotive history of my kind. Here is an extract:

> *Lift you high*
> *Above the earth*
> *Tough, beautiful Araucaria*
> *From the southern heights,*
> *Tower of Chile,*
> *Crown of the green domain;*
> *Pavilion of winter;*
> *Ship of fragrance ...*

Neruda said, he recognized the Pehuenche or Pewenche tribe as stewards of the Araucaria. Interestingly, Pehuenche, means 'people of the Araucarias' (pehuen = Araucaria, che = people). Mapuche (Pia's tribe), means 'people of the land' (Mapu = land, che = people).

Alfredo Meliñir, a leader from Quinquén, (a Mapuche Pewenche community) said, "It's a tree God left on earth, for us, the Pehuenche." Fighting against changes in logging laws (1989) he added, "In the end, we would rather die than give up defending this tree."

Ara says,
"Humans can be emotive creatures."

You, Dear Reader

So, the next time you see me standing strong; on a country estate, as you drive or walk by a private garden, in a pot in a nursery or garden centre, think of: my history and this story, the great botanists and gardeners who brought me to you and let my spirit talk to yours.

Perhaps you could also get involved with some of the conservation charities for threatened trees, and help my descendants to withstand some of their devastations. We would love to be downgraded from the Endangered category of the The International Union for Conservation of Nature (IUCN) Red List of Threatened Species.

They have suffered greatly by felling, conversion of native forest for grazing pastures, and seed collection. Though the Chilean government have put in laws (1990) to reduce this, it still happens. We are vulnerable to forest fires particularly in habitats with recurrent volcanism. During 2001-2002, over 20,000 hectares of native Araucaria forest were dramatically burnt in southern Chile affecting more than 50% of Araucaria forest in Tolhuaca National Park and Malleco National Reserve.

Ladey has promised to give donations to the International Conifer Conservation Programme (ICCP) from the sale of this book, but do look into this programme yourself.

Ara says,
"Humans can be Araucaria friends."

**Earth provides enough
to satisfy every man's needs,
but not every man's greed.**

Mahatma Gandhi

Part Two

In Love with the Monkey Puzzle Tree

**What we are doing to
the forests of the world
is but a mirror reflection
of what we are doing to
ourselves and to one another."**

Chris Maser
*Forest Primeval: The Natural History
of an Ancient Forest*

In Love with Monkey Puzzle Trees

This part of the book shares with you additional material about the Araucaria and the people who have made the Monkey Puzzle Tree part of their lives.

My Araucaria writing journey started with the inspiration of Denis' love for the tree, then I began to jot down key ideas and the skeleton of the story evolved including narration through the eyes of the Araucaria Tree herself. After this, it was researching and this hasn't stopped! As with most book ideas, I didn't know what I didn't know!

From an article on line, I discovered David Gedye, the Araucaria Guru, and his definitive book on the Monkey Puzzle Tree. In due course, my signed book arrived with a personal note asking about my interest in the tree. There was an invitation I couldn't resist and we began an email correspondence. I adore authors who engage with their readers.

From small kernels, saplings grow... it wasn't long before I'd arranged to meet up with David, at a gardening club talk. Then I asked him to write a foreword for this book and we've become friends.

I've corresponded with other writers of books dedicated to the Chilean Pine: Rodrigo Fernández and authors who describe the Monkey Puzzle Tree within their own fiction novels or memoir.

16 December 2021

Dear Ladey

Thank you for purchasing a copy of "Araucaria the Monkey Puzzle". It was while researching the trees my great-great-grandfather cared for at Dropmore that I came to realise that much of the credit given to Veitch and Lobb for the Monkey Puzzle's introduction was misplaced and that the role of others, such as the Horticultural Society and their collector, James Macrae, had been ignored. I also felt the story of Menzies sourcing his seed at a meal with the Viceroy of Chile was probably more myth, than reality. This realisation and my forebear's involvement in with the earliest trees to reach Britain, was my motivation to research and write "Araucaria the Monkey Puzzle", a book in which I give credit for the tree's introduction to those to whom I believe it truly belongs. But there is much more to the Monkey Puzzle than just the story of its introduction. I hope you enjoy reading the myriad of other information about the tree, and the wider Araucariaceae family of trees, as much as I enjoyed researching this iconic tree and the history of its arrival into Europe.

You may like to know that I have gifted the original photograph of the Archibald Menzies Monkey Puzzle at Dropmore (see page 81) to Kew Garden's library archives where it can be seen and used by future researchers.

After covering the printing and distribution costs, all proceeds from book sales will be donated to the International Conifer Conservation Programme.

Sincerely, David

Ladey meeting David Gedye in person for the first time. As one of his fans this was a wonderful moment!

Modern Stories

Bruce Roberts, Author of The Godot Orange

My cousin, Jane Brown, posted pictures of an Araucaria in the grounds of Holme Lacy House in Herefordshire, where she was staying - I bet this is the most photographed Monkey Puzzle tree at the Warner Leisure site.

There was one down the road from me. I will have to take a walk past and see if it's still there.

Patricia Frost, Businesswoman

I love the Monkey Puzzle trees. I often wondered how they got their name. I had a lovely one in my garden in Spain. I was totally traumatised one day when I returned to the house to find the tree being cut down by my then partner deciding it was blocking the sun! He is now an ex-partner!

Feel free to contact Ladey with your own Ara Story, photograph or picture.

Ladey Adey

Hergest Ridge, Herefordshire

In Love with the Monkey Puzzle Trees

Gerry O'Brien, Author of Wildlife Whispers

I remember a beautiful summers evening stroll we took up Hergest Ridge in Herefordshire, where there is a random copse of Araucaria. It seems so out of place amongst the wild expanse of the rolling hillsides but also strangely comforting.

We stopped and absorbed their presence for quite a while and my daughter, Aoife, swung around the lower branches. I remember remarking, *"You reminded me of a monkey"* and Aoife questioned how the tree got it's name, so she'll enjoy this Ara tale.

As we later passed back by the trees, with the sun going down, suddenly they seemed quite fitting in the landscape and not out of place as on my initial impression. Perhaps the trees had spoken to us!

Alison Snookes - Sleaford

In the 1970's, there was a monkey puzzle tree on Grantham Road, Sleaford. My sister, Janet, and I loved it as it was so unusual. However, subsequent owners chopped it down, maybe it was getting too big for the small front garden.

Whereas, Castle Causeway in Sleaford, right next to the river, has a thriving Monkey Puzzle Tree. At one time, the people who lived in the house had a pet monkey in a cage at the bottom of the garden, which could easily be seen when passing the house. I always felt very sorry for it and have no idea how they came to have a monkey as a pet. The monkey has not been there for a long time but the tree survives!

Ladey Adey

Angela Wodehouse Pickersgill

Lovely to have met you at Harrogate flower show. It is with pleasure I send you some pictures of the monkey puzzle trees at Sewerby Hall and Gardens near Bridlington. In 2018, a few trees were lost but the staff at Sewerby were inspired and wood carver, Allen Stichler, was commissioned to make some large plaques with quotes on for displaying in the gardens from the fallen 1868 tree. It is believed it was grown, on site, by Yarburgh Lloyd-Greame, owner, from seeds he brought back from his trip to South America in the early 1860s.

Sewerby Hall Gardens, Bridlington

In Love with the Monkey Puzzle Trees

Myth, Superstition or Fact

Morriston Monkeys

The people from Morriston, Swansea, Wales are often called Morriston Monkeys and one reason could be for the number of Monkey Puzzle trees they had at one time. A new tree has recently been planted but there is only one original left!

Steffan Phillips

Chairman of the Friends of Morriston Park

Here is Steffan's take on Morriston Park history. *"The first story I heard was from my grandparents. It was to do with what was known as the Monkey Parade. Boys and girls would go to the cinema on Saturday nights and afterwards walk up and down the streets and look at each other, it would be a place where people would meet.*

Some people have suggested the monkey term attached to the parade was not people being rude about the youth of Morriston but because of the trees (there were loads of them around Morriston), but it might be something to do with both. The exact reason we don't know. Some people get very angry when it is suggested this is anything to do with the Monkey Puzzle trees. I've always thought it was nice to have both explanations."

www.walesonline.co.uk/lifestyle/nostalgia/people-morriston-known-monkeys-16970614

Ladey Adey

Monkey Town

The accolade for the name Monkey Town is claimed by a small, south-east Lancashire town called Heywood according to this website giving its history. www.heywoodhistory.com/

The name has nothing to do with our wonderful tree but the accent of those brave Irish railwaymen constructing the railway lines in the late 1840s. There was an influx of Irish refugees into Lancashire due to the Great Famine. With lots of Irish accents they would say, *"Heap Bridge"* but it sounded like, *"Ape Bridge"*. Monkeys had only just arrived in Britain, so would have be a topic of conversation. From Apes to Monkey Town, the nickname stuck and adding to the folklore the locals would joke about Heywood men having tails and the stools and benches had a hole not for carrying but for the men's tails to fit through!

Shhh when passing a Monkey Puzzle Tree

Many Mums and Dads told their children to be quiet as they passed the tree. They believed they would have bad luck or lose something. Some creative parents would tell their kids to be quiet else they may grow a monkey's tail! Obviously, equally creative children would shout as they passed a tree as they wanted a monkey's tail!

A belief from Cambridgeshire has Monkey Puzzle trees being planted on the edge of graveyards to PREVENT the Devil from climbing them and then watching burials.

In Love with the Monkey Puzzle Trees

One widely-shared bit of folklore is, the Devil himself sits in this tree and people have to be quiet when walking past or else they will attract the Devil's attention and get bad luck for as long as three years.

In 2019, a ten year Monkey Puzzle Tree was stolen from the graveyard of Old St Michaels in Crieff, Strathearn. I wonder if the thieves have experienced bad luck since digging it up!

Stories grow as a way to protect children, after all fairy tales like *Little Red Riding Hood* have been told to give the message about the danger of talking to strangers for centuries. Monkey Puzzle myths could be seen as today's parental health and safety management! We would not want our 'little monkeys' to get hurt by spiky pine needles as they try to climb them.

This is a better way than a Council's solution to chop down the landmark 150 year old Monkey Puzzle tree at West Cross because they feared children's safety (or being sued by parents!). They said, *"It is part of health and safety, as the tree with its needle-like points of its leaves are deemed a danger to children"*. The local paper's headline was, *"150 year old Monkey Puzzle tree for the chop because council says its needles are 'like syringes'.*

Thankfully, after residents mounted a campaign, after several months, a final decision was made for the tree to remain and alternative health and safety measures put in place.

Ladey Adey

The Marmite® Tree

Do you love or loathe the Monkey Puzzle tree? Those who suffer from Araucana dendrophobia are definitely in the latter camp. It's the name given to the phobia of the Araucaria tree.

Mandy, told the author, *"I have no idea how it all started but now I have a panic attack everytime I come across a Monkey Puzzle tree. When I walk past one, my heart rate goes up, I can't breathe, I tremble and sweat uncontrollably. Although I hate them, I have a curious fascination and have to look at them."*

I am sure Ara would respond in this way. For those suffering from this phobia, all I want to do is put my branches gently around them without prickling and say, *"I love you and all humans"*.

I guess it's the last thing they would like me to do. It makes me very sad but I send much empathy, as if I had a specific anxiety and dread it would be Pyrophobia - a phobia about fire! I hope one day, everyone will be able to appreciate my beauty without fear.

Beauty in the Eye of the Beholder

It might also be a case of Beauty is in the Eye of the Beholder as the late environmentalist and journalist, Dick Warner was not a fan. He entitled his popular column in the *Irish Examiner*, **'No riddle: monkey puzzle tree is just ugly'**. He described the tree, *"They have bark like the skin of an elderly elephant, leaves which look like the scales of a venomous reptile, and the shape of the tree is disturbingly extra-terrestrial. Some trees are more beautiful than others, but the monkey puzzle is the only one which is invariably ugly."* He goes on to give his view of the Araucaria in Ireland, *"The Irish climate bears* *some resemblance to that of the Andean plateaux, which are the monstrosity's natural home. As a result, we have some of the finest specimens outside South America. If you want to avoid them, then don't visit places like Powerscourt in County Wicklow or Woodstock Gardens in County Kilkenny."*

Desmond Clarke, Irish author and professor of philosophy at University College Cork (UCC) visited Chile in 1964 and came across the trees in the wild. He wrote: *"...it came as a shock to see those weird forms looming through the mist ...edging the plateau above the Laguna Malleco like sentinels in a lost world, I once again had the impression of something very remote and ancient... the Araucaria is always an impressive tree...*

...In a garden it is like an elephant in a circus..."

Charlotte Raffo, Businesswoman

My parents planted a monkey puzzle tree when I was born. As I grew up, I had pictures in my school uniform and fancy dress taken with it.

Then it got MUCH bigger than me! It had cones for the first time in the year I got married, and baby trees appeared around its base the year I had my first child.

Sadly, once the tree got to about 40 years old it had to be taken down as it was growing into the roof, and one of its branches had taken a 'bite' out of the guttering.

I named my business after it, partly so the tree would live on, but also because many characteristics of the tree aligned with my business. They are quirky, unusually beautiful and resilient.

My Monkey Puzzle Tree business creates award-winning wallpapers and fabrics with a twist and a conscience; bringing art and character to interiors.

Ladey Adey

William Moult

The Monkey Puzzle Tree Harvest

This written account is about The Monkey Puzzle Tree Harvest featured in *The Steel Crown*, the official publication of the North American Araucanian Royalist Society (NAARS). It provides reliable English-language information about the history of the Kingdom of Araucania and Patagonia, the current activities of the Royal House of Araucania, and reports regarding the Mapuche people.

Every January 25th, the families of the valley gather to celebrate the Nguillatun. A summer festival-cum-prayer meeting which is nonstop for three days and nights. Quinquen about 100 miles east of Temuco in the region of Araucania.

Moult gives detailed description of the people and the celebration and the author likes to think of Pia as one of the woman, dressed up and celebrating the tree.

It takes place before the trees produce their fruit and early in the mornings during the Nguillatun time is set aside for praying. At this time, all present would kneel down or stand facing the young monkey puzzle tree, recite prayers, place sacred objects and relics at the base of the tree.

Each family in the valley had its own area of trees where they go to collect the nuts.

William Moult is a member of the NAARS. He spent time with the Peheunches and Mapuches working for Television New Zealand and the Discovery Channel.

Read the full article: www.araucanie.com/naars/The%20Steel%20Crown.htm

Monkey Puzzle in the Arts and Literature

Grace Stacey

I will Meet You Under the Monkey Puzzle Tree (Extract)

...The monkey has many tales to tell.
As the swaying branches of the tree resists.
Not one of them, in anyway true to the winds.
Unlike shifting hues, of the sky,
Or the mood prevailing,
Blatantly, from the Moors.
I will meet you under the monkey puzzle tree,
Only, because you seem to know no better...

Fiorella Angelini

The Araucaria Project: My Journey to Discover The Sacred.

In this 36 minute film, Fiorella investigates the Araucaria in the UK. It blends a documentary and poetic style, showing its origins, arrival to UK and its relationship with its indigenousname.
https://araucariaproject.com

Ladey Adey

Rodrigo Fernández

Chilean Native Tree Araucaria in the Wild

This incredible three minute video is shot by filmmaker, Rodrigo Fernández about the Monkey Puzzle in its environment. The cinematography is incredible and Rodrigo is one who knows how to create an environment for his vision. He draws in the audience as we go on a journey with him looking at all aspects of the Araucaria araucana in Chile. Aerial shots frame the trees showing their beauty on screen. Watch it here: https://vimeo.com/685049395

Aerial View of Araucaria

In Love with the Monkey Puzzle Trees

Recommended Books

David Gedye

Araucaria The Monkey Puzzle

How the Monkey Puzzle made its way from Chile to Europe and become a favourite of Victorian gardeners.

The love of this tree is in David's genes! An incredible relationship passed down through generations. Unfortunately, there are only few copies available and it is likely this book may soon be out-of-print, though Version 2 is promised! David has kindly offered this link of his original research:

www.dendrology.org/publications/dendrology/the-introduction-of-araucaria-araucana-into-the-british-isles/.

Sage Press

Monkey Puzzle

This sweet hand sized pocket book is part of the *Collector's Series of Trees*. It brings together the facts and stories in a super way. From a survey, they unravelled a multitude of stories including, Monkey Puzzles given as wedding presents, one grown in a Slate Quarry in Oswestry, Shropshire and Disneyland Paris buying a collection of Monkey Puzzle trees from Longleat House, Bath.

Ladey Adey

Stephen Gillen

The Monkey Puzzle Tree

An Inspirational Story of Transformation and Redemption, (From the Troubles in Belfast to the Heart of London's Organised Crime Scene.

In his memoir, Stephen says, *"The monkey puzzle tree stood proud, unmoving and alone.*

My uncle used to tell me a wonderful fantasy as a child. How curved streets had giants buried under them... and never speak in front of a monkey puzzle tree. Be careful of what you are thinking when you are close to it, especially what you say! They can live to be a thousand years old. As old as some of the mountains in these parts. They have a secret language. But they are truly magical. It is said the Monkey Puzzle Trees hold all the secrets of the land... but beware, for they are so loyal, so silent that whoever they hear speak loses the gift of speech and can never speak again!

... I was always in awe of it."

A further chapter is dedicated to the mystical form of the Monkey Puzzle Tree in a dream like narrative. (Winner of the People's Book Prize).

Callyn Journal Press

Monkey Puzzle Tree Journal

This is a 150 page lined notebook but with a lovely front cover of guess what? Yes, an Ara.

In Love with the Monkey Puzzle Trees

Three Rivers District Council

The Very Puzzled Monkey Puzzle Tree

This book celebrates the history of Leavesden Country Park, Hertfordshire.

Author *Jess Hodges*, former Park Ranger at Leavesden Country Park was inspired to write about these magnificent specimen trees which stand proud in the Edwardian Garden.

The book tells the story of 'Martha', a monkey puzzle tree, and the journey of these trees to the UK. The beautifully written narrative shares with the reader Martha's many questions about the tree's name, heritage and their very spiky branches! The character of Martha and her inquisitiveness has been brought to life in a series of uniquely illustrated drawings by Leanne Coelho. Copies were given to pupils of local schools. Available online www.threeriversleisure.co.uk/the-very-puzzled-monkey-puzzle-tree

Little Unicorn Discovers the Dinosaurs

This book written by Ladey Adey and Abbirose Adey features the Monkey Puzzle Tree in the graphics. The hand drawn picture is featured numerous times and it took Abbirose over 13 hours to draw it.
https://www.ladeyadey.com/buy-books/

Ladey Adey

Rodrigo Fernández

Chilean Trees around the World

This book is a selection of sixty stories from around the world, encompassing some fifty Chilean trees species and over three hundred pictures. Each one of the stories confirm the knowledge and appreciation shared by many foreigners have of Chilean trees. It is a ten year research by the author and numerous Chilean and international collaborators. Today the book can be enjoyed by specialists, as well as people with a simple curiosity in botany. The stars are the Chilean trees, but the protagonists are also the places, the stories of how the trees were planted there and the people with which they coexist.

Jonathan Drori

Around the World in Eighty Trees

This book is beautifully illustrated by Lucille Clerc, and is about eighty different trees species and their intricate relationships with people, animals and other plants. The book combines history, science and a wealth of quirky detail giving us all surprises. Can you find Ara?

Jonathan still makes short films for plant and seed-collecting expeditions and is also known for several TED talks.

Watch here www.ted.com/speakers/jonathan_drori

In Love with the Monkey Puzzle Trees

John Gribbin and Jeremy Cherfas

The Monkey Puzzle

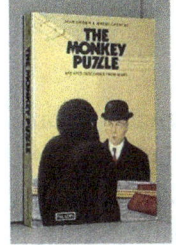

A book exploring evolutionary science and looking at the origins of humans. The prologue pays homage to the Monkey Puzzle Tree. *'Evolutionists describe the relationships between species in terms of a many-branched bush or tree of life. By a happy coincidence there is a kind of tree which is popularly known as the monkey puzzle tree. A favourite tree of Victorians, described in one book as 'rather unfriendly', these have extremely sharp points that curve back along the branch, and would have posed quite a problem to any monkey wishing to climb to the tasty nuts at the branch tips. (Why Victorians saw this as a problem we do not know, for there are no monkeys in the monkey puzzle's native forests.)"*

Myra Cohn Livingston

Monkey Puzzle and Other Poems

A collection of poems about trees found in various parts of the United States, from the white birches of New England to the Sierra redwoods on the Pacific coast and of course a Monkey Puzzle tree.

Muriel Spark

The Ballad of Peckham Rye

This 1960 novel may be making a comeback! It's main character, Dougal Douglas, was said to be associated with the Devil and had shape-shifting abilities, and in one scene he adopted the form of a Monkey Puzzle tree.

R A Dick

The Ghost and Mrs Muir

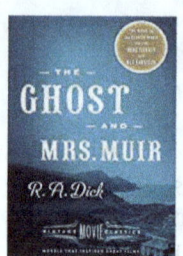

This story has several incarnations, as a book, radio play, theatre, film and TV series. R. A. Dick is a pseudonym for Josephine Leslie. Sadly, it features the demise of a Monkey Puzzle tree.

'Lucy Muir, burdened by debt after her husband's death moves to Gull Cottage in the seaside village of Whitecliff. The house is haunted by former owner and sea captain Daniel Gregg. The two form a special friendship but all is not well when Lucy makes changes around the cottage.

"Lucy hired a gardener to come and cut down the Araucaria. The Captain burst on her consciousness like a whirlwind that evening.

"My tree - my monkey-puzzle tree - I planted it with my own hands!" he stormed.

"Why did you?" asked Lucy.

"Why! Dammit, because I wanted a monkey puzzle tree in my front garden" replied Captain Gregg.

"But why?" persisted Lucy. "It's not useful and it's certainly not ornamental..."

Martin F Gardner, Paulina Hechenleitner Vega and Josefina Hepp Castillo

Plants from the Woods and Forests of Chile

From authors who have travelled extensively throughout Chile and have great knowledge of the Araucaria araucana. This book has sensational illustrations and is beautifully arranged.

In Love with the Monkey Puzzle Trees

James McCarthy

The Monkey Puzzle Man - Archibald Menzies Plant Hunter

A fascinating biography into the life of Scotsman, Archibald Menzies. Menzies was appointed as naturalist to accompany Captain George Vancouver on HMS Discovery, a four year voyage around the world. When the surgeon fell ill, Menzies took over his duties. Menzies' mentor and benefactor Sir Joseph Banks, wanted him to concentrate on botany which in itself caused quarrels with Vancouver. Menzies collected many specimens of plants including the Araucaria, alongside animals and birds, bringing them back to the UK for collectors.

James McCarthy has researched the correspondence between Banks and Menzies alongside Menzies own journal to give this biography character.

Sonia Tilson

The Monkey Puzzle Tree - A Novel

The Monkey Puzzle Tree is mentioned throughout the novel.

'They pulled up near the front door, under a very different sort of tree. Gillian stared at it, her stomach still queasy from the long drive. It didn't seem like a proper tree at all. It looked dark, almost black, its branches like giant bottle brushes sticking out at crazy angles. All wrong somehow.

"Look!" said the mother taking out the suitcases "A monkey puzzle tree! How unusual! Isn't that nice!"

Ladey Adey

Joanne Rand

Song: The Monkey Puzzle Tree

Musician Joanne has written and recorded a song about *Meeting Under the Monkey Puzzle Tree* - what a romantic place to meet. Here is the chorus:

*And I'll meet you
Under the monkey puzzle tree.
We will keep dry
and the world will let us be.
I can see you
and I know you see me
and I'll love you
under the monkey puzzle tree.*

Listen to it here on this link, www.joannerand.bandcamp.com/track/the-monkey-puzzle-tree-2

David Trewin

David is a woodturner from Cornwall who specialises in producing beautiful pieces from Araucaria timber. He makes, bowls, vases, light pulls and wooden pens. This is what he says about using the Monkey Puzzle Wood to create table lamps from trees which have died or are storm damaged.

"My bowls and vases are partly turned as soon as possible after obtaining the tree, they are then left to air dry for a period of 2-3 years, before being returned to the lathe and shaped to a high quality finish using Danish Oil."

David brings part-finished items into his home to make sure the wood is dry and accustomed to room temperature. www.turning-wood.com

In Love with the Monkey Puzzle Trees

PUBLIC HOUSES

England

**The Monkey Puzzle
30 Southwick Street,
Off Sussex Gardens,
Paddington,
London,
W2 1JQ
020 7723 0143**

**The Monkey Tree
Gin Bar and Restaurant
8 Mill Lane Mews,
Ashby-de-la-Zouch,
Leicestershire,
LE65 1HP
01530 560222**

**Monkey Puzzle
Leatherhead Road,
Chessington,
London,
KT9 2NE
01372 744 060**

Monkey Puzzle
101 Ively Road,
Cove,
Farnborough,
GU14 0LE
01252 546654

Monkey Tree
70 Bridgford Road,
Rushcliffe,
West Bridgford,
Nottinghamshire,
NG2 6AP
0115 666 0333

New Look at 2022.
Now Changed to the Giggling Squid but the Monkey Puzzle Tree is still there.

Monkey Tree Holiday Park
Scotland Road,
Newquay,
TR8 5QR
01872 572032

In Love with the Monkey Puzzle Trees

Wales

Puzzle Tree
The Watton,
Brecon,
Powys,
Wales,
LD3 7EG
01874 610005

The Monkey Tree Bar & Grill
564 Neath Road,
Morriston,
Swansea,
SA6 8HE
01792 702656

Spain

Araucaria Restaurante,
Calle Real de la Plaza,
7 35330 Teror,
Spain
928630918
www.facebook.com/
restaurante.araucaria.teror

Canada

Monkey Tree
4025 Boren Street,
Victoria,
British Columbia,
Canada, V8X 2E9
250 727 3550
www.monkeytreepub.ca/

The author, Ladey and her daughter, Abbirose Adey enjoyed a drink at the Monkey Puzzle in Paddington and had a great chat with the staff. Apparently, they have collected the kernels in the past and cooked them, though they didn't have enough to make it a dish of the day on the menu!

Ladey & Abbirose visiting Monkey Puzzle Pub, Paddington

In Love with the Monkey Puzzle Trees

WEBSITES WORTH SEEING

Araucaria araucana National Geographic Wild
www.youtube.com/watch?v=tUeWahDamws

Ladey says, "A gorgeous, two minute video with beautiful cinematography taking us through the seasons."

Chile Travel - Everything you need to know about the Araucaria, the National Tree of Chile
www.chile.travel/en/uncategorized/everything-you-need-to-know-about-the-araucaria-chisel-national-tree-2

Ladey says, "Everything it says in the title."

Indigenous peoples save Chile's Araucaria Forest Global Ideas
www.youtube.com/watch?v=JoDTKnVSBMg

Ladey says, "Perhaps Pia's descendants? Giving the history of the Mapuche Tribe, ecosystems and how and why they collect Araucaria Pine Nuts."

Yolanda Vanveen
Growing Your Monkey Puzzle Tree
www.youtube.com/watch?v=plNtu6j1WHE

Ladey says, "A simple method for growing a Monkey Puzzle Tree - plant it and enjoy it!"

Lyn Kimberley - Desert Plants from Avalon
www.youtube.com/watch?v=WQ7t2qb6yuY

Ladey says, "Lyn provides indepth information about growing the Araucaria, presented in a clear and easy to follow manner. Lyn is also a cactus fan."

Robbie Blackhall-Miles
www.theguardian.com/lifeandstyle/gardening-blog/2015/may/07/monkey-puzzles-araucaria

Ladey says, "The sadness of the article tells of a fire in Chile's China Muerta National Park losing 1,000 year old trees. Robbie includes his personal story."

The Gardens Trust
www.thegardenstrust.blog/2021/12/04/the-puzzle-of-the-monkey-puzzle

Ladey says, "Great blog with a picture of a monkey on the tree! Super plates in history and extracts from the Gardener Chronicles in 1841."

Larry Hodgson
www.laidbackgardener.blog/2016/11/08/the-monkey-puzzle-tree-curious-indeed

Ladey says, "Fun facts from the late Larry Hodgson, how to grow and how this 'living fossil' sometimes thrives or sometimes dies!"

In Love with the Monkey Puzzle Trees

Mark Griffiths
www.countrylife.co.uk/gardens/curious-questions-how-the-monkey-puzzle-tree-get-its-name-211369

Ladey says, "The Country Life article (Feb 8th 2020) which started my correspondence with David Gedye."

Max Zytaruk
www.youtube.com/watch?v=mOZLJobNwL8

Ladey says, "Max enthuses over an Araucaria and gives a great description, expressing the wonder of the tree."

Fintry, Stirlingshire - Araucaria growers
www.monkeypuzzleworld.co.uk/

Ladey says, "A beautifully put together website by Monkey Puzzle enthusiasts featuring photos of trees in Scotland, up-to-date information on pollination and other facts."

Alys Fowler and Jane Perrone
www.theguardian.com/lifeandstyle/gardening-blog/audio/2015/may/07/sow-grow-repeat-podcast-trees

Ladey says, "Robbie Blackhall-Miles is interviewed on the Sow, Grow and Repeat gardening podcast regarding the scarcity of the Monkey Puzzle Tree and how we can help."

**Nature is not a place to visit.
It is home.**

Gary Snyder

MONKEY PUZZLE FUN

Just the name Monkey Puzzle makes me smile, so here is a chapter with some FUN. It includes information which didn't seem to fit anywhere else, recipes and puzzles to solve. Answers on page 70. Enjoy.

Scientific Classification

Kingdom:	Plantae
Phylum:	Tracheophytes
Division:	Pinophyta
Class:	Pinopsida
Order:	Araucariales/Pinales
Family:	Araucariaceae
Genus:	Araucaria
Species:	Araucaria Araucana

So now you know!

Ara's Other Names

Araucaria imbricata
Candabra Tree
Chile Pine
Chilean Pine
Cook Pine
Désespoir des Singes
(The Monkey's Despair)
Dropmore Tree
Living Fossil Tree

Molina's Pine
Monkey Puzzle Tree
Monkey Tail Tree
Pehuén Tree
Piñonero
Sir Joseph's Banks's Pine
The King's Tree
The Marmite® Tree
Windsor Tree

Ladey Adey

Seed in the Hand

Photograph by Nicolás Encina on Unsplash

Monkey Puzzle Fun

Araucaria Recipes

The main thing is if you can find a recipe for pine nuts you can replace these with Araucaria seeds or Monkey Puzzle nuts. The hardest challenge is to find the nuts themselves! Apart from foraging in your own or friendly owner's garden and taking your life in your hands to get the kernels – there is no obvious source.

Blogger, Urban Huntress, has a super article, Foraging - Monkey Puzzle Nuts, www.urbanhuntress.com/2013/09/11/foraging-monkey-puzzle-nuts-2/

Should you be lucky enough to find some seeds, then the easiest way to cook them is 'toasting' them in a frying pan with about a tablespoon of oil. Fry them for a two-three minutes and as they are exotic, give them a couple of tosses. You only need a couple of minutes as they burn easily and should not be left alone. Put in a salad or the dish you plan.

You will be using gymnosperm, yes it does sound fun doesn't it, - it means naked seed. Some have suggested cutting the tip off or cutting in half so they slide out of the outer skin. Enjoy and send the author a photo.

Hugh Fearnley-Whittingstall has a recipe on his website: Summer Couscous with Monkey Puzzle nuts, www.rivercottage.net/recipes/summer-couscous-with-monkey-puzzle-nuts/

Jared Rydelek - Weird Explorer, video is a Monkey Puzzle Seeds Review and Pesto Recipe (Araucaria araucana) - Amazing Plants
www.youtube.com/watch?v=NchD65sQoEw

Ladey Adey

ARAUCARIA ARAUCANA

How many new words (3 letters or more) can you find using the letters from our favourite tree?

1   6

2   7

3   8

4   9

5   10

JOKES

What did the Monkey Puzzle tree do when the bank closed?
It started its own branch.

How do Monkey Puzzle trees get online?
They log in.

Why did the Monkey Puzzle Tree need to take a nap?
For rest.

Can you climb a Monkey Puzzle tree?

Maud Woodcock wrote in the journal, *The Tree Lover*, Spring 1941, "It wasn't climbing up the tree which was a problem but climbing back down, due to direction the spines grow!"

David Gedye's book shows an old photo (1970) of a man who climbed an Araucaria. It took him a couple of weeks to be free from the spines which stuck in him!

Monkey Puzzle Fun

CODEWORD

Codewords are crosswords with no clues! Instead, every letter of the alphabet has been replaced by a number, the same number representing the same letter throughout the puzzle. All you have to do is decide which letter is represented by which number!

5	7	11	11	13	14			19	14	10	18	14		15
14								14				12		8
26		8	21	8	7	4	8	21	24	8		1		25
14	8	21		21				25			5	24	16	14
16		19		1		4	2	24	13	14		16		22
4	7	14				9		16		10		4		25
2		16		4		25		8		14		1		8
14		1		9		17	9	1	8	16	18			4
		24		16				14				22		21
25	9	16	6	14	18					22		5	24	8
24		8				6 **K**		3		9		24		14
16				18	14 **E**	8	21		8		6		
10	8	23	24	10		26 **W**		9		21	9	18	8	13
				9				22						9
20	7	14	14	16	23	24	4	1	9	21	24	8		19

A B C D E F G H I J K L M N O P Q R S T U V W X Y

1	2	3	4	5	6 **K**	7	8	9	10	11	12	13
14 **E**	15	16	17	18	19	20	21	22	23	24	25	26 **W**

Ladey Adey

MAZE

Can you help the monkey find it's way to the Monkey Puzzle tree in the middle?

The Araucaria Cruciverbalist

Rev John Galbraith Graham was a cruciverbalist – a crossword compiler, for *The Guardian* and *Financial Times* newspapers from the 1950s. He used pseudonyms. For the Guardian it was Araucaria and his pen name for the Financial Times was Cinephile. His grave sits in a quite Cambridgeshire village of Somersham, and his gravestone has the inscription, *John Galbraith Graham ('Araucaria') Priest.*

Monkey Puzzle Fun

AN ARA TO COLOUR

JOKE

What is a Chilean Pine tree's favourite radio station?
Any which play the poplar hits especially those by Spruce Springsteen.

Ladey Adey

God doesn't leave his puzzles halfway finished...

Philippians 1:6 *(NIV Bible)*

INTERNATIONAL CONIFER CONSERVATION PROGRAMME

The International Conifer Conservation Programme (ICCP) was established at the Royal Botanic Garden Edinburgh (RBGE) in 1991. It combines taxonomic, conservation, genetic and horticultural research with international capacity building to further conifer conservation.

Over the last 27 years, they have worked in more than 50 countries around the world, focussing on Chile, New Caledonia, Lao PDR, Vietnam, China and other parts of Southeast Asia.
www.rbge.org.uk/science-and-conservation/genetics-and-conservation/conifer-conservation/

Conifer's conservation status was changed to 'Endangered' by the International Union for Conservation of Nature (IUCN) in 2013 due to the dwindling population caused by logging, forest fires, and grazing.

Martin F. Gardner, was the Coordinator of the International Conifer (1991-2021) and is most knowledgeable about Chilean Native Flora (he has travelled many times to Chile and written several books; his most recent is *Plants from the Woods & Forests of Chile* (which includes some extraordinary illustrations of Araucaria).

A percentage of the royalties from this book will be donated to the ICCP whose mission is:

'To explore, conserve and explain the world of plants for a better future.'

Ladey Adey

**And I dream of the vast deserts,
the forests, and all of the
wilderness of our continent,
wild places that we should protect
as a precious heritage for our children
and for our children's children.
We must never forget that it is
our duty to protect this environment.**

Nelson Mandela

ABOUT THE AUTHOR

This is Ladey's thirteenth book and came to her as she awoke one morning at 4.30 am during Betwixtmas – the period between Christmas and New Year! She couldn't wait to write it down and use the wonderful Araucaria picture her daughter Abbirose had slaved over whilst putting together the illustrations for their book: *Little Unicorn Discovers the Dinosaurs*.

Ladey is an award winning author and has been featured on the ALLi blog and in other's books, including Michael Heppell's *17 The Little Way to Get a Lot Done* and Louise Third's *PR on a Beermat*. She is the host of the Ladey Adey Show, a podcast all about books https://shows.acast.com/ladeyadeyshow.

Ladey heads up the family-run publishing business called Ladey Adey Publications, mentoring ambitious business people, poets, children's authors and other writers to publish their books. This includes a programme for dyslexic writers. She invariably has her own book in production.

When not writing, or publishing, you can usually find her in the garden, talking to God and doing activities including brick laying, dry stone walling, or creating mosaics. She loves to listen to and watch musicals. Her favourites are,

The Greatest Showman and
Disney's Frozen I and II.

Ladey Adey

Ladey says, *"I design and build features in my garden, it's always open for visitors - especially if you arrive with cuttings or seeds from your own garden! (Consider this a genuine invite). This is me. I would love to speak with you about your author journey."*

Ladey Says,
"We are never too old to ride a Carousel."

Contact Ladey if you would like help writing your book - Authors Mentoring Programme and Self-Publishing Consultancy.

Website:	www.ladeyadey.com
Email:	ladey@ladeyadey.com
Facebook:	www.facebook.com/ladey.adey.3
Instagram:	www.instagram.com/lady_adey
LinkedIn:	www.linkedin.com/in/ladey
Pinterest:	www.pinterest.co.uk/LadeyAdey
Podcast:	shows.acast.com/ladeyadeyshow
Twitter:	twitter.com/lady_adey
You Tube:	www.youtube.com/user/LADEY2/videos

Founder: World Online Networking Day - 29th October

www.t4s.site/worldonlinenetworkingday/home

Book Academy: Come and join us - check out the website.

About the Author

OTHER BOOKS BY LADEY

1. *God's Gifts: What are the Gifts and Fruits of the Holy Spirit and Where to find them in the Bible*, (2013).
2. *Unfrozen: How to Melt your Heart from Life's Disappointment, Disillusionment and Discouragement by Opening the Door and Stepping into God's Warming Light*, (2015/17).
3. *Colouring 101: The Ultimate Guide for the Colouring Addict,* Co-Author with Abbirose Adey, (2016).
4. *Colours of Unfrozen: Reflecting, Relaxing and Rejoicing: A Believer's Colouring Book for Adults,* Co-Author with Abbirose Adey, (2016).
5. *Colors of Unfrozen: Reflecting, Relaxing and Rejoicing: A Believer's Coloring Book for All Ages,* Co-Author with Abbirose Adey, USA Ed, (2016).
6. *Little Unicorn - What's Your Name?,* Co-Author with Abbirose Adey, (2018).
7. *Start Writing Your Book Today,* e-book, (2019).
8. *Little Unicorn and the Nativity,* Co-Author with Abbirose Adey, (2019).
9. *Little Unicorn Discovers the Dinosaurs,* Co-Author with Abbirose Adey, (2020).
10. *Successful Business Networking Online,* (2020/22).
11. *Your Path, Your Way to Successful Networking,* with Kaplan International Pathways, Book 1, (2021).
12. *Your Path, Your Way to Successful Networking,* with Kaplan International Pathways, Book 2, (2022).

Ladey Adey

Answers to Puzzles

Codeword and Maze

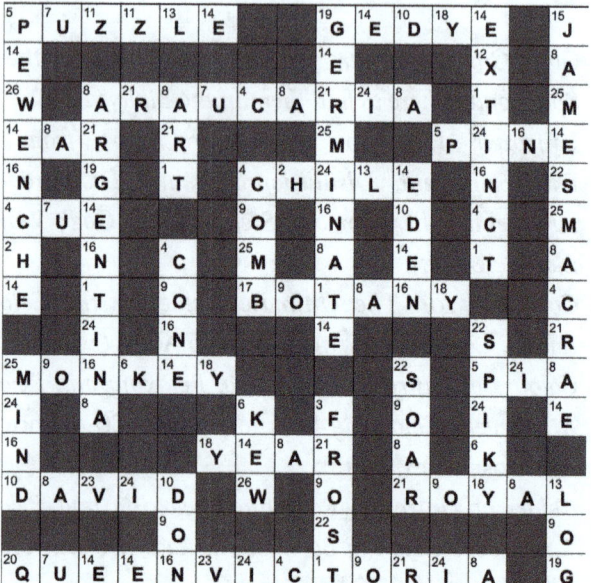

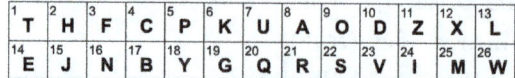

Index

A

Adey, Abbirose , 67, 69, 52, 69, 69, iv
Adey, Denis Peter v, 27
Andes 16
Angelini, Fiorella 39
Ara xii, 3, 4, 5, 6, 7, 8, 9, 10, 11, 12, 13, 14, 15, 16, 17, 18, 19, 20, 21, 22, 29, 31, 36, 42, 44, 57, 23
Araucana Dendrophobia 36
Araucariaceae 57
Araucaria Imbricata 57
Araucariales 57
Austin, Charles 14

B

Banks, Joseph Sir 9, 47
Benmore Estate, Scotland x, 19
Blackhall-Miles, Robbie 54, 55
British Isles 10
Brown, Jane 29
Buckingham Palace 11, 15
Bunya Bunya Tree 3

C

Callyn Journal Press 42
Candelabra Tree 57
Cape Horn 16
Carlton House 12
Carousel 68
Carter, John 21
Castle Causeway, Sleaford 31
Cherfas, Jeremy 45
Chestnuts 9
Chile 8, 9, 10, 16, 17, 53, 54
Chilean Geranium 10
Chilean Pine 57
Chile's China Muerta National Park 54
Chile Travel 53
Clarke, Desmond 37
Clerc, Lucille 44
Codeword 61, 70
Coelho, Leanne 43
Colouring 101 69
Colours of Unfrozen 69
Cook Pine 57
Country Life 55

D

Dendariarena, Francisco 8
Désespoir des Singes 57
Dick, R A 46
Diplodocus 3
Disneyland Paris 41
Disney's Frozen I and II 67
Dombey, Joseph 8
Dowager Queen Adelaide 17
Dropmore, Buckinghamshire 11, 13, 15, 18, 28, 57
Dropmore Tree 57
Drori, Jonathan 44

E

Einstein, Albert 2
Encina, Nicolás 58

F

Fearnley-Whittingstall, Hugh 59
Fernández, Rodrigo ii, 27, 40, 44

Financial Times 62
Fintry, Stirlingshire 55
Ford, Mary 14
Fowler, Alys 55
Frost, Patricia 29
Frost, Philip 18, 19

G
Gandhi, Mahatma 24
Gardner, Martin F 46, 65
Gedye, David iii, vii, x, xii, 19, 27, 41, 55, 60
Gillen, Stephen 42
God's Gifts 69
Graham, John Galbraith, Rev 62
Great Exhibition of 1851. 15
Great Famine 34
Grenville, Lord and Lady 11
Gribbin, John 45, 46
Griffiths, Mark 54

H
Hamond, W 21
Heap Bridge, Heywood 34
Hechenleitner Vega, Paulina 46
Hepp, Castillo, Josefina 46
Heppell, Michael 67
Hergest Ridge, Herefordshire 31
Heywood, Lancashire 34
Hill, Matthew 21
HMS Blonde 10
HMS Discovery 47
Hodges, Jess 43
Hodgson, Larry 54
Holme Lacy House, Herefordshire, 29
Horticultural Society 28

I
INIA 17
International Conifer Conservation Programme (ICCP) 65

J
Jefferson, Robert 21
Jesus 7, 15
Jokes 60, 63

K
Kernels 9
Kew Gardens, London 9, 10, 12, 17
Kimberley, Lyn 53, 54
King William IV 11, 17
Klinky Tree 3

L
Laguna Malleco 37
Leavesden Country Park, Hertfordshire 43
Leslie, Josephine 46
Little Unicorn and the Nativity 69
Little Unicorn Discovers the Dinosaurs 19, 69
Little Unicorn - What's Your Name? 69
Living Fossil Tree 57
Livingston, Myra Cohn 45
Lloyd-Greame, Yarburgh 32
Lobb, William 16, 28
Loddiges 17
Longleat House, Bath 41
Lucombe & Pince 17

Index

M
Macrae, James 10, 28
Mandela, Nelson 66
Mapuche Tribe 38, 53
Marmite® 36, 57
Maser, Chris 26
Maze 62, 70
McCarthy, James 47
Menzies, Archibald 9, 10, 12, 28, 47
Mesozoic 3
Molesworth, Sir William MP 14
Molina's Pine 57
Monkey Puzzle Tree v, 14, 19, 57
Monkey's Despair 14, 57
Monkey Tail Tree 57
Morriston 33, 34, 51
Moult, William 38

N
National Geographic Wild 53
Neruda, Pablo 22
Nguillatun 38
North American Araucanian Royalist Society 38

O
O´Higgins, Ambrosio 9
O'Brien, Gerry 31
Old St Michaels, Crieff 35
Oswestry, Shropshire 41
Owen-Hughes, Sarah ii

P
Paleozoic 3
Pangea 3
Peheunche Tribe 38
Pehuén 6
Pehuén Tree 57
Pencarrow Estate, Cornwall 14
Perrone, Jane 55
Phillips, Steffan 33
Pia 6, 53
Piñonero 57
Pinophyta 57
Pinopsida 57
Plantae 57
Podcast 68
Powerscourt, County Wicklow 37
Prince Albert 15
Public Houses
  Araucaria Restaurante, Spain 51
  Monkey Puzzle, Chessington iii, v, 49, 50, 59
  Monkey Puzzle, Farnborough iii, v, 49, 50, 59
  Monkey Puzzle, Paddington, London 49, 52
  Monkey Tree, Canada 49, 50, 51
  Monkey Tree Holiday Park, Newquay 50
  Monkey Tree, West Bridgford 49, 50, 51
  Puzzle Tree, Powys iii, v
  The Monkey Tree: Ashby-de-la-Zouch 49
  The Monkey Tree Bar & Grill, Swansea 51
Pyrophobia 36

Q
Queen Victoria 15
Quinquen, Temuco 38

R

Raffo, Charlotte 37
Rand, Joanne 48
RBGE 65
Rembrandt 84
Robert Jefferson 21
Roberts, Bruce ii, 29
Royal Academy of Arts 13
Rydelek, Jared 59

S

Sandwich Islands 10
Sewerby Hall, Bridlington 32
Shaw, Doris v
Sierra Redwood 45
Sir Joseph's Banks's Pine 57
Skirving 17
Snookes, Alison 31
Snyder, Gary 56
Spark, Muriel 45
Stacey, Grace 39
Start Writing Your Book Today 69
Stichler, Allen 32
Successful Business Networking Online 69

T

The British Library iv
The Gardener's Chronicle 18
The Greatest Showman 67
The Guardian 62
The Horticultural Society 10
The King's Tree 57
Third, Louise 67
Tilson, Sonia 47
Tracheophytes 57
Tremlett, Captain 21
Trewin, David 48

U

UK Forestry Commission 17
Unfrozen 69
University College Cork (UCC) 37

V

Vancouver, George, Captain 47
Vanveen, Yolanda 53
Veitch 16, 17, 28
Veitch, Robert T 17

W

Warner, Dick 36
Wenham, Joanna 17
West Cross, Swansea 35
Whitby Jet 15, 20, 21
Windsor Tree 57
Wodehouse Pickersgill, Angela 32
Woodcock, Maud 60
Woodstock Gardens, County Kilkenny 37

Y

Yew 15
Youells 17

Z

Zytaruk, Max 55

Your Notes

A space for your notes, to record the Monkey Puzzle Trees (ARA) you have seen - include the date you saw Your Ara and its location.

Ladey Adey

Notes of Monkey Puzzle Trees You Have Seen

Ladey Adey

Notes of Monkey Puzzle Trees You Have Seen

Ladey Adey

Notes of Monkey Puzzle Trees You Have Seen

Ladey Adey

Notes of Monkey Puzzle Trees You Have Seen

Ladey Adey

**Choose only one master
- nature.**

Rembrandt

www.ingramcontent.com/pod-product-compliance
Lightning Source LLC
Chambersburg PA
CBHW070001300426
43661CB00141B/113